DISASTER SCIENCE

FLOODS

BY NAOMI CAMERON

Gareth Stevens
PUBLISHING

Please visit our website, www.garethstevens.com. For a free color catalog of all our high-quality books, call toll free 1-800-542-2595 or fax 1-877-542-2596.

Cataloging-in-Publication Data
Names: Cameron, Naomi.
Title: Floods / Naomi Cameron.
Description: Buffalo, NY : Gareth Stevens Publishing, 2027. | Series: Disaster science | Includes glossary and index.
Identifiers: ISBN 9781482482041 (pbk.) | ISBN 9781482482058 (library bound) | ISBN 9781482482065 (ebook)
Subjects: LCSH: Floods--Juvenile literature.
Classification: LCC GB1399.C364 2027 | DDC 551.489--dc23

Published in 2027
Gareth Stevens Publishing
2544 Clinton Street
Buffalo, NY 14224

Portions of this work were originally authored by Marne Ventura and published as *Detecting Floods*. All new material in this edition was authored by Naomi Cameron.

Designer: Joshua Olson
Editor: Claire Vanden Branden
Content Consultant: William Gallus, Professor, Department of Geological and Atmospheric Sciences, Iowa State University

Photo Credits: Cover, p. 1 Artiom Photo/Shutterstock.com; p. 4 Dan Thornberg/Shutterstock.com; p. 7 US Coast Guard; p. 8 Zelideth Rodriguez/US Air Force/DVIDS; p. 10 aerogondo2/Shutterstock.com; p. 13 LaiQuocAnh/Shutterstock.com; p. 15 Eye Travel/Shutterstock.com; p. 16 Dewitt/Shutterstock.com; p. 19 Marcin Szymczak/Shutterstock.com; p. 21 Dennis MacDonald/Shutterstock.com; p. 23 NOAA; p. 25 Farizul H./Shutterstock.com; p. 26 DreamArt123/Shutterstock.com; p. 29 Lazy_Bear/Shutterstock.com.

Printed in China

CPSIA compliance information: Batch #QS27GS: For further information contact Gareth Stevens at 1-800-542-2595.

TABLE OF CONTENTS

CHAPTER 1

SUDDEN FLOOD

On July 3, 2025, a storm moved toward Hunt, Texas. The Guadalupe River flowed nearby. It had a history of flooding. So, the National Weather Service (NWS) issued a flood watch for the area. Just after midnight on July 4, rain began to fall. At 1:14 a.m., NWS sent out a **flash flood** warning.

The Guadalupe River is about 250 miles (402 km) long.

Between 2:00 and 3:00 a.m., almost 2.5 inches (6.4 cm) of rain fell. The river began rising quickly. By 3:15 a.m., it had risen almost 3 feet (0.9 m). And in the next 30 minutes, it rose nearly 6 feet (1.8 m) more. By 4:00 a.m., the river was raging.

Rain continued to fall hard. Between 4:00 and 6:00 a.m., the river rose even more. Many areas flooded. By 7:00 a.m., police began to **evacuate** people from the area. But for many, it was too late.

In just a few hours, the Guadalupe River had risen to 37.5 feet (11.4 m). The flash flood tore through Kerr County. Many people's homes were wiped out. Cabins disappeared. Cars were swept away.

Kerr County was hit the hardest by the Guadalupe River flooding.

The rushing flood caught many people by surprise. The flood engulfed an all-girls summer camp, Camp Mystic. Dozens of campers woke up to danger.

Teams used dogs to help with rescue efforts after the Guadalupe River flooded.

Emergency response teams rushed to flooded areas. Survivors clung to trees as they waited to be rescued. Some waited on the roofs of their homes. But not everyone could be saved. More than

160 people went missing in the flood. And more than 130 people died. This included 27 campers and counselors from Camp Mystic. The flood was the sixth-deadliest in US history.

FLASH FLOOD ALLEY

Unfortunately, the flood on July 4, 2025, was not the first in Kerr County. The county is part of an area in Central Texas known as "Flash Flood Alley." In the past 100 years, the Guadalupe River has flooded more than 42 times. Some of these floods are deadly. One example took place in 1987. The river rose 29 feet (9 m). Ten teenagers died.

CHAPTER 2

UNDERSTANDING FLOODS

People, plants, and animals on Earth need water to live. Most of the planet is covered with water. When the sun heats the water, some of the water **evaporates**. The water rises, cools, and forms clouds. When the water droplets in clouds grow big enough, they become raindrops and fall back down to the planet's surface.

Heavy rain falling into rivers is one of the main causes of floods.

The movement of water back and forth between the surface and the **atmosphere** is called the water cycle.

Falling rain enters oceans, lakes, and rivers. It may also flow on the surface and soak into the ground. Flooding occurs when an area gets more water than it can handle. Storms can bring too much rain. Melting snow in the spring can dump extra water into a river. When this happens, rivers overflow. The soil can't soak up any more water. Water collects and flows on the surface.

The flat lands along the sides of rivers are called floodplains. When rivers overflow, these strips of land hold

Melting snow can fill up rivers and cause flooding downstream.

the water. However, floodplains are usually dry. So people often build cities there. Being near the river is useful most of the time. Rivers make travel and trade easier.

But these cities are at risk when floods happen.

Deltas are land areas where a river empties its water into the ocean. **Sediment** builds up in deltas. This makes the soil very fertile, or good for growing plants. People who live in deltas are at risk of floods.

CITIES IN FLOODPLAINS AND DELTAS

Throughout history, towns and cities have sprung up near water for many reasons. People need clean water to live. The fertile soil in deltas and floodplains is good for farming. Traders use boats to send goods to other places. And the land near rivers is easier to build on because it is flat.

The Mississippi River Delta is the largest delta in the United States.

Some floods happen slowly, after many days of rain. Flash floods occur quickly, in a few hours or less. Heavy rains brought by severe storms or hurricanes can cause flash floods. Other times, flash floods happen because a **dam** or **levee** breaks.

CHAPTER 3

PREPARING FOR A FLOOD

People build levees to prevent floods. Levees are barriers built along the sides of a river. They are usually made of soil. They raise the banks of the river so it will hold more water. This stops the water from flowing into nearby towns. The Mississippi River has levee systems built along its banks in some areas.

When levees work properly, they can protect wide areas from flooding.

Dams are another way that people control the flow of water. Dams are walls built in rivers. They are often made of concrete or soil. They slow the water's flow. This forms a lake, or reservoir, behind the wall. Dams can prevent flooding. Sometimes they also use the force of flowing water to create electricity.

Government officials send out flood warnings when they know a storm might cause flooding. People in high-risk areas can check the internet, TV, and radio for information. This gives them time to prepare. They might want to put sandbags around their homes to block the water. Or they might move to higher places.

Dams allow people to collect, store, and control huge amounts of water.

If the flood risk is high, officials might tell people to evacuate. Officials can warn people that certain areas, such as deserts, are more likely to have flash floods in a sudden rainstorm.

Hurricane
Forecaster
LX4
XT4
DELL
DELL

CHAPTER 4

PREDICTING FLOODS

Meteorologists are scientists who study weather. They use computers, **radar**, and other technology. They look for weather patterns. They make predictions about storms, hurricanes, and floods.

For example, one way that meteorologists predict floods is by using radar. Radar data can tell scientists where rain is falling.

Radar data helps meteorologists figure out where floods might happen.

Radar can also show which way the wind is blowing and how fast a storm is moving. Meteorologists track the path of the storm. This lets them predict where the storm will go next so they can warn people who may be in its path.

Scientists also use weather satellites to detect floods. Satellites orbit Earth. They take photos of the atmosphere.

DOPPLER RADAR

To track storms, Doppler radar stations send out radio waves that bounce off rain, hail, or snow. Scientists can measure how long it takes the waves to return. The technology is named for Austrian scientist Christian Doppler.

Satellites track floods and other dangerous weather events.

Meteorologists use this information to predict floods.

Computer models are another way to predict flooding. Scientists feed data from radar and satellites into computers. The scientists add data about how much water a floodplain can absorb. They also factor in how heavy a rainfall or snowmelt is. A computer program combines all this data into a model of the situation. Scientists use this model to find how likely a flood is in a certain area.

Computers also help engineers design stronger dams and levees. Engineers use math to figure out the best shape, weight, and height for these structures.

Designing and building new dams is one way to reduce flood risks.

Oroville Dam is an embankment dam in California. It was built in the 1960s to help control floods.

Dams come in several styles and shapes. An embankment dam is the most common type. It looks like a large wedge or hill. It is made by piling up rock and soil. Engineers choose soil types that won't let much water through. Other dams are made from concrete. For example, gravity dams use thick walls to hold back water.

Scientists use data to find the safest places to put dams. They also use computers to monitor the structures after they are built.

Scientists can often predict and detect floods. With enough warning, people can protect their homes or evacuate to dry areas. Floods may damage property, but detecting them early can help keep people safe.

FLOOD SAFETY

There are several things you can do to stay safe during a flood. The most important thing is to stay out of the water. Even just 6 inches (15 cm) of moving water can knock you off your feet.

If you live in an area where floods may happen, prepare an emergency flood kit. Pack a flashlight, batteries, and food. You should also include clean drinking water and first aid supplies.

Check the internet, TV, or radio for alerts. A flood watch means there is a chance a flood could occur. A flood warning means that flooding has already started or will start soon. If your area is under a flood warning, move to higher ground right away.

In an evacuation, local officials will send out instructions. It's important to follow these

People may pile sandbags to help protect their homes from floods.

instructions right away. Don't return home until officials say the area is safe. And when you return, watch out for **debris** and other dangers.

TEST YOUR KNOWLEDGE

Take this quiz to test your knowledge.

1. Write a letter to a friend describing what you learned about ways to prevent floods from happening.

2. Do you think people should build cities on floodplains? Why or why not?

3. What is the water behind a dam called?

   A. a reservoir
   B. a delta
   C. a floodplain

4. What do sandbags and dams have in common?

   A. They can both be used to generate electricity.
   B. They can both be used to block flood waters.
   C. They can both be built quickly to protect a house.

Answers can be found on page 32.

GLOSSARY

atmosphere
The layer of air that surrounds Earth.

dam
A wall that stops water from flowing.

debris
The remains of something broken.

evacuate
To leave a place of danger.

evaporates
Changes from liquid to gas.

flash flood
A sudden rush of water caused by heavy rain.

levee
A structure built next to a river to stop floods.

radar
A device that sends out radio waves for detecting and locating objects.

sediment
Stones, sand, or other material that is carried by a river's rushing waters.

FOR MORE INFORMATION

BOOKS

Alderman, Christine Thomas. *Floods*. Mankato, MN: Black Rabbit Books, 2021.

Becker, Trudy. *Floods*. Mendota Heights, MN: Apex Editions, 2026.

WEBSITES

Britannica Kids: Flood
kids.britannica.com/kids/article/flood/353136
Find out more about how and why floods happen.

National Geographic Kids: Floods
kids.nationalgeographic.com/science/article/flood
Learn more fascinating facts about floods.

Publisher's note to educators and parents: Our editors have carefully reviewed these websites to ensure that they are suitable for students. Many websites change frequently, however, and we cannot guarantee that a site's future contents will continue to meet our high standards of quality and educational value. Be advised that students should be closely supervised whenever they access the internet.

INDEX

Answer Key: 1. Answers will vary; 2. Answers will vary; 3. A; 4. B